Kanban

The Ultimate Guide to Kanban Methodology for Agile Software Development

© **Copyright 2018**

All rights Reserved. No part of this book may be reproduced in any form without permission in writing from the author. Reviewers may quote brief passages in reviews.

Disclaimer: No part of this publication may be reproduced or transmitted in any form or by any means, mechanical or electronic, including photocopying or recording, or by any information storage and retrieval system, or transmitted by email without permission in writing from the publisher.

While all attempts have been made to verify the information provided in this publication, neither the author nor the publisher assumes any responsibility for errors, omissions or contrary interpretations of the subject matter herein.

This book is for entertainment purposes only. The views expressed are those of the author alone, and should not be taken as expert instruction or commands. The reader is responsible for his or her own actions.

Adherence to all applicable laws and regulations, including international, federal, state and local laws governing professional licensing, business practices, advertising and all other aspects of doing business in the US, Canada, UK or any other jurisdiction is the sole responsibility of the purchaser or reader.

Neither the author nor the publisher assumes any responsibility or liability whatsoever on behalf of the purchaser or reader of these materials. Any perceived slight of any individual or organization is purely unintentional.

Contents

INTRODUCTION 1
WHAT IS KANBAN? 2
KANBAN AND SOFTWARE DEVELOPMENT 8
KANBAN BENEFITS 12
KANBAN AND LEAN 16
KANBAN GOALS 20
STEP-BY-STEP GUIDE 25
KANBAN BOARD 34
MAPPING THE VALUE STREAM 42
KANBAN AND DEADLINES 45
THE SEVEN KANBAN CADENCES 47
ANALYTICS AND METRICS 52
WIP LIMITS 57
HELPFUL TIPS 59
CONCLUSION 69

Introduction

You could start to test all different types of methods for project management, but that will take too much time, and can be tedious. Though you may learn a lot from all of your experiments, when it comes down to getting things done, you need to have the most efficient method. You can still use the old standbys of test-driven development, pair programming, and planning poker. A lot of people discovered that Scrum had a huge impact on their productivity; that was, until they found Kanban.

Production teams have found that every minute they use Kanban has added value to their products and for their customers. They don't waste any time or effort, and they know their work is quality work.

This book is here to introduce you to this amazing system. You won't have to do any experiments or go through any mishaps. All you have to do is follow the information and then reap the rewards of the Kanban system. Don't wait and allow your competition to find this information first. Make use of the Kanban system and reap all of the benefits this management system can bring.

What is Kanban?

The Kanban system is a system used to schedule just-in-time manufacturing and lean manufacturing. In Japanese, Kanban literally means billboard or signboard. A Toyota industrial engineer, Taiichi Ohno, came up with Kanban to increase their manufacturing efficiency. The name was derived from the cards the factory used to track production. For those that work in the automotive industry, Kanban is known to all as "Toyota nameplate system." This is the reason why other automobile manufacturers don't want to use the term Kanban.

Kanban immediately became useful in helping support a production system and promoting further improvement. The system is used in finding problem areas by measuring lead times and cycle of the process and its steps. The biggest benefit of Kanban is that it creates upper limits to work in process inventory to prevent overcapacity.

One of the main goals of the system is preventing excess inventory buildup within the production areas. Limits are placed on items stored at supply points. Once inefficiencies are identified, the limits are reduced and then eventually removed. When limits are exceeded, the identified inefficiency will be taken care of.

History

The Kanban system originated from an empty box which was just a simple replenishment signaling system. The UK Spitfire factories first developed this during the war, and they referred to it as the "two-bin system." Then, in the late '40s, Toyota began to search supermarkets to look for shelf-stocking methods to use on their factory floor.

When it comes to grocery stores, customers will typically get what they need at the needed time. Furthermore, customers only take what they need, knowing there will surely be a future supply. This is why grocery stores only stock things expected to sell at a particular time. Noticing this, Toyota started to compare a process to a customer from previous processes, as well as the previous processes to a store.

Kanban is used to align the levels of inventory with consumption. There will be a signal indicating that a specific material was already consumed, and the supplier now needs to deliver a new shipment. The replenishment cycle will track these signals, which will bring visibility to the buyer, supplier, and consumer.

The demand rate is what Kanban uses to control the production rate. The demand is passed from the very last buyer up to the store processes. In 1953, Toyota used this new idea in their machine shop.

Toyota Operations

A demand forecasting needed a push, which is why production scheduling was a success. On the contrary, Kanban approaches by pulling from the demand, before the ordering the product. Production and re-supply will be figured out based on customer orders.

When the supply time becomes too long, and the demand is still uncertain, the best thing to do is to quickly respond when a demand is noticed. The Kanban system excels this way. The Kanban system acts as a demand signal which will quickly make its way to the supply chain. This will ensure better management and smaller amount of the intermediate stock in the supply chain. When the response to supply is slower than the demand fluctuations, which causes a possible lost sale, building of stocks may be appropriately considered. Kanban is then added to the system to reach the required stocks.

Taiichi Ohno explains that for a Kanban system to be effective, it has to follow strict rules. Toyota came up with a list of six rules. They have to constantly monitor those rules, which will ensure that their Kanban system does exactly what it needs to.

The six rules that Toyota formulated for their Kanban application are:

1. All processes will provide a request to its supplier as the supplies are consumed.
2. All processes are produced based upon the sequence and quantity of incoming requests.
3. Without a request, nothing will be made or delivered.
4. The request is always attached to the item.
5. Processes have to ensure that they only deliver defect-free items.

6. Pending requests should be limited to make sure that the processes are sensitive and determine the inefficiencies.

Cards

The Kanban cards help in signaling the movement of the materials as well as in switching materials from the outside supplier to the main production facility, making it a very important part of the Kanban system. This card is like a message showing the depletion of parts, products, or inventory. When Kanban receives the message, it will trigger the replenishment of that particular part, product, or inventory. The consumption will trigger the demand for additional production, while the card will prompt the demand for products. In simpler terms, the Kanban cards produce a system driven by demands.

In terms of lean production proponents, they have always believed that demand-driven systems will lead to lower inventory levels and quicker turnarounds. This ends up helping companies be more competitive by implementing these types of systems.

Systems that use Kanban signals have become increasingly popular over the last couple of years. This new trend has reduced the usage of Kanban cards. However, it is still commonly used in modern production facilities. Kanban uses email notification in signaling demand to the suppliers. It can also be used in various kinds of software systems. A "Kanban trigger" will be activated when a specific part has hit a lower amount than the number that was indicated on the card. It will demand a purchase order with set quantities to the suppliers. The supplier then needs to fulfill the request within the specified time.

While the Kanban cards have stuck to the primary principles of Kanban, it still needs extra materials. There's a need for more parts if an empty bin contains a red card.

Three-Bin System

The simplest example of the Kanban system is the "three-bin system." This is used when there is no in-house manufacturing of supplied parts. Their initial demand point is the bin found on the floor of the factory. The inventory control point is the bin located in the factory store. Finally, the supplier has the last bin. The classic Kanban cards are removable cards found in each bin which contain the details and other important facts about the product.

Since the parts inside the bin positioned on the factory floor are used for manufacturing and are often empty, the bin, along with its Kanban card, is sent to the store. The store will replace the emptied bin with a full one that also has its own Kanban card. The empty bin will then be sent out to the supplier from the factory store.

The supplier will eventually give its product bin with card back to the factory store. The empty bin is now at the supplier. This is the final step in the process, meaning it will never run out of the product. It can also be considered a closed-loop process. This is because it only provides the exact amount of the product needed in a single bin without worrying about oversupply. The spare bin will allow for any uncertainties in supply, transport, and use. The best system will compute enough Kanban cards for each product. The heijunka box, a colored-board system, is commonly used in many major factories.

Electronic

Several manufacturers have started to use an electronic Kanban system, which will help to reduce the common problems like lost cards and manual entry errors. Electronic systems can be used in enterprise resource planning systems, which will enable real-time demand signals throughout the supply chain as well as improve the visibility. Tracking the supplier leads and the replenishment times from the date taken from the electronic system can improve the levels of the inventory.

Functioning as a signaling system, the Electronic Kanban uses a combination of technology in triggering the movement of the materials, both in the manufacturing and production. The use of technology such as barcodes differentiates this kind of Kanban from the original, which still uses cards and email messages.

Inventory is typically marked with barcodes, which a worker uses at the process' various stages to signal usage. Messages are sent out through the scans to the external and internal stores to ensure that the products are restocked. The messages are routed to the suppliers through the internet. The inventory can also be viewed in real time.

Organizations like Bombardier Aerospace and Ford Motor Company have improved their processes using electronic Kanban systems. You can see widespread use of these systems from bolt-on modules or single solutions to ERP systems.

Systems

Adjacent upstream and downstream workstations talk to each other within the Kanban system through their cards, where all bins have an associated Kanban. An important part of this is Economic Order Quantity. The more popular types of Kanban systems are:

- Transportation Kanban – This authorizes the transport of a full bin to a workstation downstream. This is also found in the bins that are connected to the transportation to move throughout the loop again.

- Production Kanban – Once received, this Kanban authorizes a station to make a definite number of products. The containers associated with it carry this Kanban.

Kanban and Software Development

You know how Kanban got started, and how it was meant to be used. Now, let's look at how it can be helpful in software development. Let's begin by looking at the differences in the planning process between different agile methodologies.

Differences between Scrum and the Kanban methodology:

- Kanban contains no timeboxes at all.
- Kanban methodology tasks are larger, and there are fewer tasks.
- It's optional to use periodical assessments in Kanban, or there aren't any at all.
- Kanban has no "speed of team." They only have an average time for full implementation.

Looking at this list, think about what will remain of the agile methodology if sprints are taken out, dimensions are increased, and you stop counting the speed of your team's work. What remains? Nothing?

How would you be able to talk about any supervision over development if you get rid of all the major tools?

Managers like to think they have to be in control all the time. Their supervision over the development process doesn't exist. If a team isn't interested in working, it is going to fail a project despite any control level.

If a team enjoys their work and works with complete efficiency, then you don't need control. The control will only disturb the process and increase the cost.

For example, one of the most common problems with Scrum is the higher costs because of discussions, meetings, and time lost at the joints of the sprints. At the very least, a day is used to complete a sprint, and another to begin another sprint. If you have a two-week sprint, then two days out of those two weeks comes to 20%, which is a lot of wasted time. So when you use Srum methodology, around 30% to 40% of the time will be wasted on supporting the process, which includes daily rallies, sprint retrospectives, and on and on.

Kanban differs because it focuses on the task. When a team uses Scrum, their main objective is successfully completing the sprint. Tasks take first place in the Kanban methodology. You don't have sprints, and a single team works on a task from start to finish. Deployment will then be made when it is ready, based on the presentation of the work that has been done. The Kanban team doesn't estimate time to finish a task since it doesn't make any sense, and it's almost always wrong.

Why would a manager have to have a time estimate if they fully believe in their team's ability? Their team will work off of a Kanban board, which we will talk more in depth about later. On the board, columns to be read from left to right, may contain information like:

- Goals – This is an optional column for a board. Goals that are high-level can be added here so that everybody on the team knows about them and is easily reminded of them. Some example goals could be "Add Windows 10 support" or "20% increase of work speed."
- Story Queue – This is where all of the tasks that are ready to be started should be placed. The one with the highest priority

is placed at the top and is taken first. The card is then moved to the next column.

- Acceptance and Elaboration – This column, along with all of the other columns before "Done," will vary based upon the workflow of certain teams. Tasks that are under discussion can be added here. Once you finish your discussion, you can move the task to the next column.

- Development – This is where a task will remain until the development of the feature has been completed. Once you finish the task, it will be moved into the next column. If it turns out the architecture is uncertain or incorrect, you can move it back a column.

- Test – This is where a task lives when it is being tested. Once it has been successfully tested, it is moved into the next column. If any issues come up, then the task should be shifted back to the development phase.

- Deployment – Every project will have its own deployment. This column could mean that you put a new version on the server, or you commit the code to the repository.

- Done – The card will move to this column once it has made it through every other section on the board, and it is completely finished.

When teams use Kanban for software development, work is pulled as capacity permits. Work is never pushed into the process. This system aids in the decision-making about how much, what, and when to produce something.

The organization of a Kanban board allows for a better understanding of the workflow. It reduces waste from multitasking and context switching, shows all of the operational problems, and helps with collaboration to improve the system.

The diagrams in this book show typical Kanban board sections for workflow. The boards will vary considerably depending on the context in which they are used. The overall aim is to make the workflow and progress of individual items clear to the stakeholders and participants.

Some of the biggest companies use a Kanban system to improve their work. For example, Pixar's creative process has been heavily influenced by a Kanban system.

The President of Pixar Animation, Ed Catmull, feels it is important that their animations be made in order. This means that every team passes the product, or idea, on to the following team who will push it further down the board.

They use high-level Kanban boards to make sure that this happens. The staff that is working on a production knows exactly what they are supposed to be doing, and how their work affects their colleagues.

Spotify has also started to use a Kanban system. When it came to the Kanban board, the operations team wanted to make it as easy as possible. They have three sections: to-do, doing, done.

Their board also has two horizontal lanes. All tangible tasks, like 'upgrading data storage' are placed here, while the other lane is made up of intangible work like 'designing databases' and 'planning a server migration.'

Spotify switched to a Kanban system once they realized their workload was reactive instead of proactive. This meant that it struggled to find the time for planned projects.

They section their work into small, medium, or large tasks. The small tasks take a day, medium ones a few days, and large jobs take a week. Tasks that take longer than a week are called projects. They then split those projects up into small, medium, and large tasks. They can then place them into the backlog.

Kanban Benefits

In the early 2000s, business leaders became interested in Kanban when it was mainly used by software developers to improve workflow. Today, it has started to be used across all disciplines to help teams visualize, optimize, and manage their work.

Even science agreed on the benefits of Kanban. Visual information can be processed by the brain 60,000 times quicker than with words. Kanban kicks understanding and communication, by using visual information, into high gear.

Let's look at the several benefits your team can reap from using Kanban.

1. Versatility

The main point behind the Kanban system is communication with the use of visual signals. This benefits industries and job titles everywhere. Kanban can be applied anywhere. Any company can use Kanban either from marketing department or engineering. It's easier for projects and team members to smoothly move through various functions because of Kanban's versatility. An example of it is when moving content project to graphics from editing, or a new feature to testing from integration.

2. Continuous Improvement

Kanban's main principle encourages people to focus more on continuous improvement. Reviewing process is a lot easier due to the project management's visual system, as well as making necessary improvements to streamline workflow, remove the waste, and reduce overhead.

3. Responsiveness

Within the auto industry, where Kanban got its start, it uses process when low in inventory, creating a better method of matching demand and inventory. When used in project management, responsiveness is still a huge benefit of Kanban. With Kanban, responding to business needs in a more agile way is much easier.

4. Increased Output

The team can limit the work in progress, called limiting "WIP," using the Kanban system. Doing this, the teams are encouraged to work closely with each other in removing distractions, and multitask to finish their work. The teams can get more things done because of the improvement in intense focus and collaboration. With a more focused delivery, high-priority and high-value work items are expedited while delivering value to the business. Personal WIP limits help to relieve teams from overburdening because they can focus on a finite number of work items. They only move on to the next item in the input queue when the item that they were originally committed to is completely finished.

5. Empowered Teams

The whole team is in control of the Kanban system, and they share responsibilities for finishing the work. Kanban helps to empower the team to make agile decisions that move the project forward with efficiency and innovation. The typical siloed organizations that battle between product management and software delivery, become more integrated into the development value stream. Kanban encourages synergy between groups and helps to break down the walls between different specializations, which results in collaboration between functions. Work item transitions between columns on the board will offer opportunities for communication, collaboration, knowledge discovery, and involvement and engagement for all.

6. A Perfect Product

Projects typically make their way to the finish line with fewer reworks and errors because of the increased concentration on continuous improvement and quick-response. Quality control can now be allowed in the project management in order to give more accurate results. Looking at it from a nontechnical perspective, there are lots of activities that contribute to high-quality software, like collaborative analysis and user documentation. Even within disciplined teams, the collective behavior is controlled by rules. The policies will help to solidify the professional standards that are agreed on across the board, which includes software teams, product and project managers, and stakeholders.

7. Business Value First

Kanban is positioned to be a decisions management framework, which makes it a lot more powerful than it looks from an outsider's view. It isn't just some board hung up on the wall! It helps to promote economically-based decision-making by managing and prioritizing work based on certain economic goals. Organizations are trying to survive in fiercely competitive environments. This means that we need to execute, identify, and prioritize the most valuable work so that the business can keep afloat and ahead of the competition.

8. Visibility

An amazing thing about most organizations is the amount of work that happens under the parapet. One of the core practices of Kanban is to make invisible work visible! By using a Kanban board as an information center, as well as its other merits, it offers a holistic view of process inefficiencies, blockers, impediments, bottlenecks, and progress at one glance. Information can be easily found by not only the team members but by the external observers and stakeholders. This promotes a boundaryless flow of information across the entire organization.

9. Reduction of Wasteful Activities

The majority of project managers will focus most on the timeline instead of process queues. Timelines are a part of the manager's psyche, along with Gantt charts, spreadsheets, and other time-bound documents. They don't like to embrace uncertainty. With the reinforcement of WIP limits, a Kanban board turns into a pull-based system, which keeps a reliable amount of high-quality ideas that are delivered JIT (Just In Time), while getting rid of wasteful work and lower queues. Upstream activities like business cases, discovery workshops, and requirements gathering, take place on demand and when they have to, which forces the team to make timely decisions.

10. Sustainability

Kanban systems help to manage your work at a sustainable, smooth, and humane pace, without any uncontrollable nadirs and distressing peaks, which only causes frustration, high employee turnover, and lack of commitment. A sustainable development brings about creativity, as WIP limits help to control the pace dynamically without fear of breaking a promise down the road. This allows for innovation, addresses issues in a new way, and produces solutions with fewer issues in quality.

Kanban and Lean

During the last 20 years, Kanban, Scrum, Lean, and Agile have been steadily gaining in popularity in different industries and fields.

The Project Management Institute stated that 75% of organizations that were agile were able to meet their goals or business intent with 65% finishing on time, and 67% finishing on budget. This is higher than those organizations with low agility. In the same research study, agile organizations' revenue grew 37% faster and generated 330% more profits than non-agile companies.

Lean principles have also proven that they are effective. Thanks to using a lean approach, Dropbox was able to go from 100,000 registered users to more than four million in only 15 months. The Wealthfront Company now manages more than two hundred million dollars and processes more than two million dollars on a given day. IMVU has managed to reach 50 million registered users and now makes over forty million dollars annually.

While a lot of companies have started to implement or are leaning towards these methodologies, there is typically only a handful of people in the company who actually understand the entire process.

Other employees, especially when it comes to big companies with difficult communication, follow along with the rules without a lot of deep insight. This does not mean that they aren't good at what they do—it might even be the opposite—they could be more focused on their functional tasks.

But while they aren't aware of the basic principles, don't share the corporate philosophy, aren't ready to challenge another, or can't see the difference between Scrum and Kanban, Agile and Lean, the company isn't going to see any change in their productivity.

So how are these things different and similar? Let's see.

Agile

In 2001, Agile was officially born from the Agile Manifesto to help improve productivity in software development. But it has started to expand to other areas. A project team that chooses to follow the 12 Agile principles is considered agile. Basically, agile is time-focused and an iterative philosophy that lets a team build a produce incrementally, and deliver it in small pieces. The biggest benefit is the ability to change and adapt at any point along the way depending on corporate obstacles, market conditions, feedback, and so on. They only supply relevant products to the market.

This is the reason why an agile company tends to be flexible, adapts to changes quickly, iterates less while they implement faster, and can seize new chances as they come up. It helps to provide them with a fast decision-making process by using a flexible organizational structure and basic communication. In 2015, research among 601 IT and development professionals showed that agile is the main approach for management. And it is mainly used to enhance collaboration and improve software quality.

Lean

Lean, along with Kanban, got its start in the mid-'50s in Japan within their automotive industry. Its main purpose was to reduce loss and create a sustainable production. Lean was adapted for use in software development in the 2000s by Tom and Mary

Poppendiecks who connected it to the seven initial Lean principles and Agile philosophy.

Following along with expanding Lean to any industry, Eric Reis applied it to the start-up industry in 2008 in order to help develop new services and products in times of uncertainty. In order for a start-up to be considered Lean, they have to follow the five Lean principles created by Eric Reis.

The typical Lean company will follow a 'learn, measure, build' cycle. They will do several tests, frequently connect with their customers, understand their value, and look at its key processes to make continuous improvements. By using this never-ending cycle, a start-up will become sustainable, develop smartly, and have success. By lowering the high cost of trying to get the first customer and the even bigger cost of making the wrong product, and decreasing the technology development cycles, the Lean start-up philosophy will help new ventures to launch products that their customers will actually be interested in. This enables things to be done more quickly and at a lower cost than traditional methods, which makes start-ups less risky.

As can easily be seen, both Lean and Agile aim at achieving business goals and making their client happy with a product of the best quality. These, as well as several other shared features between these mindsets, will typically lead people to confuse the two. However, they work with different tasks and purposes, and that's the reason why it is important to create a clear line between the two.

Agile and Lean aren't methodologies. They are principles that create the basis for many different methodologies, so they are more of a mindset or philosophy.

Lean is a wider-known term than Agile because its smart approach improves all types of losses like energy, labor, and money. Jeff Sutherland also explains that Agile was created after Lean, so that means that they are closely related. Conceptually, Agile is actually a subset of Lean practices and principles, which are actually a subset of Systems Thinking.

This means that Kanban is a methodology. Kanban is a part of the Lean philosophy supported by the Japanese automotive industry. But the trick is, you can still see Agile principles within the Kanban methodology.

Kanban Goals

When using a Kanban system, you will have to come up with primary and secondary goals. These are things you will have arrive at on your own, but here are some things you should strive for.

1. Primary Goal: Better performance with process improvements that are introduced with little resistance.

Your team is likely using Kanban because you believe that it will provide a better way to introduce change. Kanban is there to change as little as it has to, so that means change with very little resistance would be the first goal.

2. Secondary Goal: Deliver with high quality.

As you know, Kanban can help you deliver every element of the recipe for success. Kanban will help you focus on the quality of your product by limiting work in 0progress. It will allow you to define policies around what you find acceptable before you can pull a work item to the next step. You can include quality criteria with these policies. For example, we could set a strict policy that you can't pull user stories into test until the other tests have passed and their bugs have been resolved. This means that we are stopping the line until the story is in the right condition to continue.

3. Secondary Goal: Control the quantity of WIP to deliver a predictable cycle time.

We all know that work-in-progress is directly connected to the cycle time and that you can find a correlation between non-linear growth and time-in defect rates. It makes complete sense that WIP needs to be kept small. It will make everybody's life easier if we agree to limit this to a certain quantity. This will end up making cycle times dependable, to an extent, and will help to keep lower defect rates.

4. Secondary Goal: Allow the team members to have a better life by improving work/life balance.

While most companies talk a lot about employee satisfaction, it is very seldom a priority. Senior managers and investors too, easily view resources as fungible and easily replaced. This shows where there is a cost-centric bias in their investment or management approach. They don't look at the huge impact on performance that comes along with an experienced and well-motivated team. Staff retention is extremely important for work. As software developers age, they start to care more about the rest of their lives. A lot of them lament about how they wasted their 20s away slaving in their office over a piece of code that didn't reach expectations.

When it comes to work/life balance, it's not just balancing the number of hours a person spends at work with how many hours they get with their family and hobbies. It also has to do with providing reliability. For example, let's say that you have a team member who enjoys art and wants to take a painting class. This is every Wednesday starting at 6:30, and runs for ten weeks. Is your team able to provide that person with the certainty that they will be able to leave the office on time every Wednesday to go to that class?

When you give your team the right kind of work/life balance, your company will appear more attractive to the local market. It gives your employees motivation, and it provides your team with energy to maintain high-performance levels for months or years. It's not true that you get the best performance from knowledgeable workers being overloaded with work. This might work in a tactical sense for a few days, but it is not going to be sustainable beyond a few weeks. It's just good business to give your team a good work/life balance by not overloading them with too much work.

5. Secondary Goal: Give your team slack by keeping a balance between demand and throughput.

While balanced demand with throughput can be used to avoid overworking your team and gives them a good work/life balance, it also causes something else. It creates slack in the value chain. Every value chain has a bottleneck. The throughput that you provide downstream is limited by the throughput of your bottleneck, no matter how far upstream it was. That means, when you balance the input demand with your throughput, you will make idle time throughout your value chain except for the bottleneck resources.

The majority of managers steer clear of idle time. They have been trained to manage for efficiency, and it feels as if changes could be made to lower costs when there is idle time. This might be true, but you also need to appreciate the power of slack.

Slack can help responsiveness to the urgent requests, and it provides bandwidth to facilitate process improvements. If you don't have any slack, team members won't be able to take the time to reflect on how their work is done and how it could be better. Without slack, they won't have time to learn more techniques that will help to improve their tooling or skills. Without slack, you won't have any liquidity in your system, so that you can respond to late changes or urgent requests. You won't have any tactical agility without slack.

6. Secondary Goal: Use a simple prioritization mechanism that slows commitment and keeps your options open.

After the previous goals have been achieved, you will have created an engine for making software. After you have this in place, it's important that you make use of it. This requires that you have a prioritization method that will maximize your value, and it will minimize your cost and risk. You need a prioritization scheme that will optimize your business performance.

A lot of schemes are simple, like "high, medium, low." This type of scheme doesn't have direct meaning for the business. The more elaborate schemes started once Agile software had developed things like MoSCoW: "Must have, Should have, Could have, Won't have." Things like feature-driven development used a simplified and modified version of Kano analysis techniques. Still, others prefer a strict numerical order for value and risk.

These schemes have the same problem. To respond to market change, you have to reprioritize. With the uncertainty of the market, it's hard to predict how things will change.

This is why you need a scheme that will delay commitments as late as possible and give you an easy question to answer. Kanban will give you this by having business owners refill empty queue slots, while they also provide reliable cycle times and due-date performance.

Now, six goals would be enough for many, but here you will get two extra goals to make sure that your Kanban system works at its peak performance.

7. Secondary Goal: Have a transparent scheme so that you can see improvement opportunities to enable change to a collaborative culture which will encourage continuous improvement.

When you provide transparency in the WIP, delivery rate, and quality it will build trust with your senior management and customers. This means you provide transparency in every area of the system when something may be finished, the quality, and how well your team works. This gives your customers confidence in your work.

Not only does it put your customers' and senior management's mind at ease, but it also provides something else. Having transparency in the process will allow everybody involved to see the effects of their work. This makes your team more reasonable-minded. Their behavior changes to improve the performance of the system.

8. Secondary Goal: Have a process that allows for high-maturity development, good governance, business agility, and predictable results.

Business leaders want to make promises to colleagues at the executive table, to shareholders, to the board of directors, to customers, and the market. They also want to be able to keep those promises.

They also know that the world is fast-paced and there will be changes. That means, they want to be able to respond to those changes quickly and take advantage of all of the opportunities. In order to achieve everything that business leaders want, there needs to be more transparency.

This all comes down to an organization operating at a maturity level of four on the Software Engineering Institute's five-point scale of maturity and capability. There are not very many organizations that have reached this maturity level, regardless of whether they have reached out for an actual SCAMPI appraisal or not. It's no wonder that the majority of senior leaders of the big tech companies are frustrated with their software team's performance.

Step-by-Step Guide

In order to get started with Kanban, all you have to start with is a large board that your entire team can see, and cards to pin on it. But we're going to look at the different areas of a Kanban system so you can better understand how it works. The next chapter will get into the nitty-gritty of making a board.

Project Management

Kanban has been modified to be used in software development in a more project management approach. With the use of Kanban in software development, continuous workflow, which is also known as value stream, can be supported.

- Value Stream: All actions needed to form a project and finish it are included here. The actions can:
    - Give the project value
    - Help to avoid waste
    - Help circumvent non-valuable information.
- Waste Elimination: This is anything that doesn't add value to your project. A Kanban system works to eliminate waste. When it comes to software development, you can have three types of waste:
    - Waste in the potential of the team
    - Waste in project management
    - Waste in code development

- Code development waste happens typically because of:
    - Partially completed work: The work that is partially completed ends up becoming unusable and outdated. This can be eliminated with modular code and iterative cycles that are completed within iterations.
    - Defects: When you are developing code, correction and retesting is absolutely necessary, and it requires resources and time. This can be removed with an updated test suite, continuous customer feedback, and completing testing during the iteration.
- Project management waste happens typically because of:
    - Extra Processes: This is unnecessary documentation that will take resources and time. This could be gotten rid of with:
        - Reviews of documentation that will make sure only necessary and relevant processes are followed
        - Preplanning of all the necessary and relevant processes
    - Code Handoffs: This means that you pass the work between different people or teams after the first person has completed their work. This could cause a lack of knowledge. You can eliminate it by keeping your wireframes and flowcharts clear and visible.
    - Extra Functions: These include the features that aren't needed by the customer. Time and effort will be wasted when you work to develop the functions that are needed for implemented features that the customer hasn't even asked for. This can be removed through continuous communication with your testers and customer involved in the gathering of the requirements. The reason is that they may visualize

scenarios better, as well as the expected system behavior.

- Team potential waste happens typically because of:
  - Task Switching: This can cause waste because of multitasking. This can be removed by concentrating on only one task with each release. The larger projects are broken down into tasks to:
    - Give a way to notice and resolve bottlenecks
    - Focus on delivered work-cycle time
    - Enable easy flow of work
    - Reduce dependencies
    - Improve visibility
  - Waiting: This is time wasted for getting information or instructions. The team is subjected to sit idly if they are not enabled to make decisions, or if the team is provided with information that takes expensive resources. This can be eliminated by letting the members of the team:
    - Make decisions in order to prevent them from having to wait for more instructions
    - Have full access to the information they need whenever they need it.

Planning Flexibility

By using Kanban, you will see improvements in your flow of work. Since you will have a visual representation of the workflow, you will notice a reduction in speed from moving one task to another. This is can be done by creating clearly marked Kanban cards, flow lanes, and clearly named columns that show the location of every item within the workflow. A task with longer duration to finish can be done without much hindrance. During this time, the tasks that are finished will continue on to the next step.

This will allow for:

- The right amount of time for longer tasks that you can't logically break down.
- Value preservation for those longer tasks.
- The effort needed for every role can be expended.
- Finished tasks can flow continuously without wasting time.

This makes planning more flexible. It will not also be boxed in.

Pull Approach

When the first team of your two teams shows better performance than the other, it probably pushes more work which is too much to handle for the other team. This can create friction between the two teams. You have to create a pull approach in order to fix this.

The pull approach can remedy this. When the team is ready to work on a project, that is the only time they can pull work. You implement a pull approach by supplying a safeguard with a limited capacity between your teams.

The primary benefits of this kind of approach are:

- Reduces wait times
- Avoids work being piled up
- Helps a team to keep a constant pace and focus on quality
- Gives resource balancing

Minimize Cycle Time

The cycle time of every task is measured, and its process is then optimized in order to reduce the cycle time.

- You will immediately identify the bottlenecks and resolve them in a collaborative manner with the team.
- To reduce having to rework things, correction loops should be considered.

Continuous Delivery

The best things that come from continuous delivery are:

- Your growing products can be delivered continuously at regular times because of short release cycles
- You will have continuous interactions with your customers.
    - This helps you understand what the customers want.
    - It keeps you from producing what a customer doesn't need.
    - You get feedback on modules delivered.
- Every release cycle has limited requirements.
    - Developers don't become overloaded with various requests. This allows them to concentrate more on delivery.
    - You won't have any half-finished work.
- Instead of starting work, the main goal is getting the work finished.
    - This will keep the aim toward providing pace and quality of your product.
    - You can send the product before the customer ends up changing their mind.
- Your workflow will be optimized from start to finish.
    - This will help in incremental process improvements.
-

Visual Metrics

Having your workflow visualized on a Kanban board will help:

- Schedule following the limits of your WIP on a workflow state.
- Assign your resources in a dynamic way based on the role requirements.
- Continually track progress and status.

Every day, and with every column, mark down how many tasks you have in them. This will give you a chart that looks like a mountain. This chart will give you the performances of the past and will let you predict future results.

This chart will give you information such as:

- The cycle time for every feature by showing the begin date and the end date.
- You can assess the quality of your growing product from a user, technical, and functional perspective at different times.
- The pace of the development can be monitored by observing the amount of completed development items and looking at each item's average time.
- You can adjust the pace of the development by computing the ratio between the development days of each completed item. This ratio can be used to guess the time of completion for items that haven't been developed, and you can adjust the plan as you need to.
- Using a collaborative session, you can adjust and evaluate the process to find the needed changes that could help to improve the quality of the product or to help the development pace.
- Resolve and identify any decisions that are not validated by looking for validated decisions' cycle times. Focus then on

fixing loops that are usually the backed-up column you can't see.

Focus and Efficiency

When you focus on your costumers' demands, the scope will become clear. The aim will be on giving the customer value.

Here is how efficiency can be achieved:

- Through continuous customer interactions, their expectations can be made focused and realistic.
- WIP makes sure that tasks are focused on.
- Using a pull approach will enable resources to finish a task at hand before a new task is ever started.
- There will be faster delivery by optimizing lead times.
- By visualizing the workflow with a board, you will draw immediate attention to bottlenecks so that you can quickly fix them.
- The team becomes accountable for their success through empowerment.

Tools

There are lots of different project management tools that use a Kanban approach. Here are just a few you can choose from:

- Kanban Tool: This uses Kanban cards, due dates, tags, swim lanes, and colors to create a Kanban board. The best features include:
    - To-do lists
    - Drag and drop tasks
    - Online documents
    - Visual project management
    - Insightful analytics
    - Online Kanban boards
- Kanbanery: This is another tool that helps your team to work more effectively together through:
    - Real-time updates
    - Work with existing systems
    - Content-rich tasks
    - Advanced reporting
    - API and several third-party apps
    - iPhone and iPad apps
    - Copying or creating task boards with templates
    - GitHub integration
- LeanKit: This tool will be helpful in a distributed environment. This can also allow access to the company's CEO, partners, customers, and to all employees.

- JIRA Software: This is an Agile tool that is created for teams of every size and shape. It has features that help with:
    - Integrated workflow
    - Add-ons
    - Workflow
    - Reporting
    - Releasing
    - Tracking
    - Value-driven prioritization
    - Accurate estimations
    - Planning
- Earliz: This software supports smart project collaboration and management.
- Targetprocess: This tool helps manage and visualize Agile projects with the natural and full support of Kanban, Scrum, or custom Agile method. Its features include:
    - Visualization of project data
    - Visibility of progress
    - Test case management
    - Custom views, dashboards, reports and cards
    - Backlog story map view
    - REST
    - iOS and Android apps

Kanban Board

There are lots of people who are starting to use a Kanban work management methodology to help visualize their workflow, whether for personal task lists or projects at work. Kanban allows teams and individuals to manage multiple projects and a task by displaying tasks on what is known as a Kanban board. With a traditional board, the tasks will move from left to right as you work toward finishing the project. Ultimately, the use of a Kanban board, especially an online one, will allow teams to stay up to date on overall project progress and task status.

This is extremely useful for teams and individuals who are looking for a visual way to manage tasks and keep the workflow process streamlined and simple. This chapter will dive further into the methodology and mechanics of using an effective Kanban board. We will also look at using two tools to create such a board: Smartsheet and Trello.

The cornerstone of the Kanban methodology is a Kanban board. It is used to help you visualize and track the work that needs to be done. It works like an information hub on all task progress and status. Since you can see all of your tasks on one Kanban board, it functions as a high-level overview of the work. This will end up helping you notice any setbacks or roadblocks and will let the team adapt as they need to.

There are a few key differences in how a Kanban board and a Scrum board work. First off, you won't have to come up with structured sprints for your tasks when you use a Kanban board as you must for a Scrum board. This means, there won't be any need to reset your Kanban board after each completed phase of a task. Instead, you will use the Kanban board for the entire duration of your project or for ongoing work as you receive new tasks.

How is a Board Used?

The best thing about a Kanban board is that it is super simple to set up and intuitive to use. The board setup is very standardized. Of course, you also have the option to customize your Kanban board so that it reflects your project's needs, but sticking to the standard Kanban board structure will help you get things started.

At the very minimum, the Kanban board will have the following three columns organized from left to right:

- o Backlog – This is the column where you will place all of the upcoming work. This is where tasks that haven't been started will be stored.
- o Work in Progress – This is all of the tasks that are currently being worked on. It's important that you stay under your determined WIP limits (covered later) to make sure that you don't end up overloading yourself or your team with work that is unrealistic to finish in a given time.
- o Completed – This is where all of the finished tasks will be placed.

All of your tasks will be placed on a card, and you will move these cards into your various columns as they make it through different phases of the work process. The main goal is that your task will always move from left to right. When you make this a priority, it will make sure that all of your work is fully completed before you go to the next step. This way, it will improve your efficiency.

To make things easy for you to get started with Kanban, you can find a lot of different online tools that will help you to make a Kanban board. Two of the most popular tools are Smartsheet and Trello. Trello is a task management tool that will let users come up with task lists and monitor their progress using a Trello board, which can be created and used like a Kanban board. Smartsheet is a web app that can be used like a Kanban board and is great for projects that are more complex.

Trello

The interface of Trello works very similarly to a regular Kanban board. You will create columns to reflect your task status, and you will move the tasks across all of the columns as you get things done.

To get things going using Kanban in Trello, you need to make your first board from scratch.

1. Select the + tab button in the upper right-hand corner to start your blank board. Now, you can create a name for your board.
2. Now, you can make your columns by typing in a column header into the 'Add a list' field that they provide. Here you can create as many columns as you want to, but you do need to create a minimum of at least three: Backlog, In Progress, and Finished.
3. Now you need to add a card to your first column by selecting add a card. Then you will type in the task in the provided field. You can either write out the basic task, or you can write in more detail. This could be due date, labels, or members. You do this by selecting the pencil icon and editing the associated tab.
    a. Labels will let you color-code your tasks if want to help to organize them even further. They also have a

colorblind friendly mode that will add texture to your cards.

b. You can choose 'Change members' to assign tasks to certain members.

c. You can choose 'Change due date' to give a task a due date.

d. You can also select copy or move the task into different lanes or columns.

e. To get a more comprehensive menu of how you can edit your card, you can click directly onto the card.

4. Now, you can repeat the previous steps and finish filling-in your task board with the rest of your tasks. You can add a card into any column directly.

5. Once you have your board setup, you will start to move the cards throughout the board. You can drag and drop to move your cards along the board as you finish your work.

6. Remember, you need to make sure that tasks are completely done before you move them into the next column. This will make sure that you don't have to double back on tasks and send them back to a previous column.

There are also additional features when using Trello. For more ways to customize your Kanban board, you can also buy Power-Ups. These are extra features and integrations that will give you even more power. Select the 'Power-Ups' button under the Menu, and you will see things like voting, card again, and calendar.

Calendar will give you an extra calendar view to see your tasks, which can be used weekly or monthly.

Card aging will age your card that you haven't acted upon recently. Once you have actively used the card, the card will be restored to normal vision. This is extremely helpful to ensure that there isn't a task that gets overlooked or continually shoved back.

Voting power-up will let the other users vote on task cards to figure out their priority or interest.

You can also set WIP limits using power-ups, which will give you the opportunity to set a limit on how many tasks can be place in the "In Progress" column. This is an automated way to ensure that you never over-commit yourself or others.

Now you are ready to share your board with the other members of your team.

1. In the upper left-hand corner, you will find a 'Private' button. The sheet will automatically set to private where only you can see it, but it can be shared with several team members, or make it public.

2. Select 'Private' and then pick the option from the menu you are given.

3. The board will now be viewable, and editable if you want, to other people. Sharing this board with all the others on your team will enable collaboration and accountability.

Trello is only one tool that will help you to create a Kanban board. You can also use the mobile app so that you will be able to keep up with your work on-the-go. However, there are a lot of other tools out there that can make a Kanban board so easy, and it's important that you try out as many as you can and pick the one that suits your needs.

Smartsheet

To start creating your first Kanban board using Smartsheet, you can start with the pre-built Kanban Sheet template.

1. Make sure that you are on the Home screen and then choose "Create New – Kanban Sheet."

2. Type in a name for your board and then select OK.

3. You can also choose "Now" to import any existing data into your Kanban board from Excel, Microsoft Project, Microsoft Excel, or Trello.

4. Your list of tasks will show up in the card view, which is one of four view types that you will find in Smartsheet. The other three are calendar, traditional grid, and Gantt. In card view, you will see four columns, which they call lanes, which are automatically labeled as: "Backlog, Planning, In Progress, and Complete." Now, you can add in the cards that you need for your tasks in the right lane.

5. Next, to add in your first card, select "+Add Card" in any of the columns on your board. You will get a form pop-up for you to edit in the information about your task, which includes assigned to, priority, size, description, and title. You will also notice that the Status will automatically be listed as the land that you chose when you added in the card.

6. You also have the option to add in relevant documents or images, or you can add in comments to the card by selecting Add Discussion or Add Attachment.

7. Now select OK. The card will be placed directly into the correct lane.

8. Continue this process for all of the tasks that you need to add to your board. Make sure that you keep your WIP limit in mind when you start adding tasks to the "In Progress" column so that you don't become over-committed.

9. In order to edit your fields, you can select "Fields" in the upper right-hand corner.

10. Un-check any of the fields that you don't want to have shown on your card. You can also choose "Add New" to include extra fields in your card.

11. To create a high-level view of all of your cards, you can collapse your cards so that they only display the title of the

tasks. This makes your board look cleaner. Select the icon located to the right of the "Fields" button to switch to a collapsed view of your cards.

12. Once a task is ready to change lanes, all you have to do is drag and drop the card to the lane it now needs to be in.

13. Any of your cards can be edited at any time by selecting the drop-down menu on the chosen task and then choose Edit.

14. You can now move through your stages of work and finish things up at your own pace. However, you need to make sure that you keep your Kanban workflow tenants in mind: don't breach your WIP limit, and only let the cards go from left to right.

15. An amazing feature of Smartsheet's Card View is being able to pivot your lanes. This is possible because you have at least two dropdown list fields for the cards, and will give you the chance to organize the lanes and see the work by criteria other than just looking at simply task stages.

16. By default, the template will organize the columns by Status, meaning start to finish.

17. Select the drop-down menu next to "View by Status" so that you can see the other options where you can sort your tasks.

18. By picking the "Size," the lanes will be organized by the size of the task instead of the status. This means that if you pivot your data, you can view through different criteria.

    a. Note: "View by" is unique for every user. This means that others that can see your sheet won't be impacted if you choose to view your tasks from a different value. Anybody that you choose to share the sheet with can view it through any setting they want without affecting anybody else.

19. Lanes can also be added to your board by choosing the "View by" menu and then choose "Edit Lanes."
20. Now, you can type in additional lanes that you want to add to your board.
21. To share your board, select the "Sharing" button. You will then be prompted to type in the emails of the people you want to share it with. You will then adjust the permissions to the right levels.

The best thing about using SmartSheets for a Kanban board is the ability to see the information on your board from different viewpoints. You can switch your view of your Smartsheet by switching between: grid, Gantt, calendar, and card.

Having this flexibility will make sure that even those people who aren't familiar with Kanban can gain some helpful insights into the work that is being done. Any changes that are made while in the other views will also be updated in the Card View. This means that your data will stay up-to-date.

Mapping the Value Stream

Before a Kanban is built, you have to come up with a value stream. Simply, a value stream is a list of steps that you need to take to make value. When you create a Kanban, the work will flow along the value stream, and this will help you to visualize the flow. This is basically going to help you come up with your Kanban board. You know how to create one, but you need to know how to come up with your tasks.

Before you get started, these are some things worth remembering about a value stream:

1. It needs to match up with actual reality as close as it can.
2. It needs to be only as detailed as needed so that you can see and understand the flow of work.
3. As contexts and understanding start to change, the value stream will as well.

Start with the End

What do you need to do?

If you are going to be in a meeting, you could:

o   Fully discuss a topic.

o   Create action items.

o   Plan a future task set.

If you are looking to get things done at home, you could:

- Delegate chores.
- Plan a vacation.
- Build a porch.

If you are at work, you could:

- Make important documents.
- Manage your staff.
- Build a new section of an airplane.

Every single example could have a completely different end-state. If you are coming up with a report, the end will likely be published. So if you were creating a value stream for creating that report, you would start with you "Backlog" and then end with "Publish." Everything in-between has yet to be figured out.

Fill In

Between your "Backlog" and "Publish" is creation. What steps do you need to take to create something? If you work backward from your endpoint of "Publish" you could have "Collation," before that could be "Final," before that could be "Second Draft," and before that could be "First Draft."

This will now give you a stream where specific sections of your report can flow through. The team that is working on the report can track every section or chapter as it travels to completion.

Some important things for you to remember are:

1. The value stream is the best guess that you can come up with of how your work will actually occur.
2. The value stream is going to change.
3. The value stream is fault tolerant

Now, you know how to come up with your own value stream to add to your Kanban board.

Importance

Value stream mapping can be used to help improve the process of your work where you have repeatable steps, and especially if there is going to be several handoffs. The majority of waste in knowledge happens when there are handoffs between team members, not the actual steps. Inefficient handoffs might not appear as bottlenecks on the assembly line, but they can cause the same effect: less productivity, workers that are overwhelmed and lower quality. Mapping the process will help you to see where these handoffs happen so that you can figure out where wait times prevent work from moving along.

A lot like manufacturing, software development follows a process that is repeatable with distinctive handoffs, and continuous delivery is needed for the collaborative effort of the team.

Making sure that you have a clear and shared understanding of the process is important for software teams. Having a value stream mapping exercise for your team will reduce handoff delays, increase delivery speed, and improve communication. It will also help to solidify the process, making sure that they have a faster and more linear flow of value to the customer.

Kanban and Deadlines

A lot of teams that are adopting Kanban are coming from an Agile background. Thinking the Agile way discourages using Due Dates. This will in turn breed unwanted behavior. By focusing on Due Dates, it causes teams to work under extreme pressure. This will often translate into shortcuts being taken in the design and testing departments. The end result is that the quality of work gets compromised and then technical debt will pile up.

Even though project teams need to be self-driven and self-organizing, in actual reality, it could be very different. Not having Due Dates might cause momentum to be lost inside the team. This is when Parkinson Law comes into play. Scheduling five days of work could easily turn into seven days if there isn't any expectation set for a five-day deadline. If the project works on a fixed budget, slippage might pile up sooner than you think. This can cause an escalation of management.

There are many situations when using Due Dates at the task level would be very useful. The main one is not talking about resorting back to old ways. This will then cause the Due Date to become a deadline that is cast in stone. Then, the technical or quality debt would become a secondary consideration. It is a very useful guideline for a team member to see when they need to complete a task at hand.

So, you must be thinking how do I set a Due Date?

The normal approach is always estimation. Kanban systems don't use detailed estimations in actual hours but utilize story points. Sometimes, hour estimates actually exist. Projects done by IT companies are estimated by bids for the pre-sales lifecycle. These estimates are figured out by a developmental team. They don't often have the same set of details. Most pre-sale estimate gets expanded to better estimates when it is time to execute.

Using a Kanban system, sizing tee shirts is communicated by whether or not a certain card needs to be finished in one or two weeks. By doing this, teams can figure out the relationship between size and the time it is going to take them to make it. This will determine the Due Date.

The Kanban system also focuses on lead and cycle time data. It creates statistical charts that help the team make commitments at different levels like card, sprint, or release level. They can do this with an air of confidence. After figuring out the amount of data historically, teams that use Kanban can set Due Date to give guidance to the team members or show stakeholder and customers a timeline.

To sum it up, you must have balance. Agile teams don't like Due Dates since they send the wrong message and result in subversive quality and behavior. Having an absence of Due Dates might cause some teams to not finish their work. While Due Dates that are driven by estimates do work well, using a Kanban system can give additional assistance to teams to help them figure out better Due Dates. You can use Due Dates along with Kanban cards, but only use them as guidelines. Do not use it to make your team compromise the quality of the product or add to your technical debt.

The Seven Kanban Cadences

One of several things that show the difference between Kanban and Scrum is that Kanban uses cadences. A cadence can be defined as a rhythm of activity. An example would be to hold a meeting to plan once every two weeks. Then when the sprint has ended, hold a review meeting. Add in some more, you will soon feel the beat of consistent productivity.

Think about having no cadences, but you still need the meetings. Things will start to fall apart. You haven't held any meeting in months. You might decide that you need to have a meeting. Someone might come to you and tell you they don't have anything to do. Someone might ask you to do a meeting. All the meetings then start to feel like it is an emergency. This doesn't make anyone feel good.

Stand-up Meeting

This is the meeting that is held the most. It helps to keep the team informed about the project. It is used to address questions such as who needs help, are there any blocked tasks, who is working on what.

This meeting gives the team information to help them make decisions about what to do with their time. It is the feedback that the team needs and helps stakeholders in knowing what is happening and if they can help in any way.

It is held with everyone standing to keep the meeting short and sweet. The format of the meeting can change drastically. It can have a round of questions going from right to left and scanning the Kanban board to look for bottlenecks and blockers.

Replenishment Meeting

Systems need to have tasks in the input queue to keep from being starved. This meeting is when the team decides what those tasks will be. This is essentially a planning meeting. The format might be different, and the number of shareholders involved will change. If your team has problems prioritizing work that comes from multiple managers, you might think about organizing bi-weekly phone conferences with everyone involved to help prioritize the work.

This is when the word 'maybe' gets turned into 'should.' It is the step between possibilities and the company's commitment point. This is when the latest information is sent in. It is determined that a set of tasks are the most important thing to put into the system. If this is done frequently, it will help the stakeholders to trust that whatever is promised will get delivered regularly.

You just need to right people to be at the meeting to make the right decisions with the best data. This type of meeting can look different. It all depends on the context. You can have these daily or just once a year. It needs to be efficient in giving feedback and how quickly it delivers. You can even hold them on an as-needed basis.

Operations Review

This is a high-level view of how the different departments, divisions, teams, are working together as an organization.

You should know how bad local optimization is. You can't improve one part of the system without thinking about the other parts. One team can't save the entire organization if it has a poor delivery. Most inefficiency happens during handoffs and queues. During this meeting, different managers will find ways to help to improve the entire system.

By using input from other cadences, managers will see how the entire company is performing. Are the clients happy? Is the company profitable? Have there been many staff turnovers? Are there departments that aren't being used? Based on all this date, the team will experiment on how they can improve efficiency and lessen variation throughout the whole system.

Delivery Planning Meeting

This meeting shows if the company doesn't deliver right to the final customer. This meeting will smooth out tasks between departments or teams.

Customers might not want to see work piled on their doorstep randomly. They like being involved in figuring out when what, and how it is delivered.

Look over the output of stand-up meetings and the entire board of data. Look at any risks that might arise during risk assessment. See what is ready to deliver and what will be ready soon. This meeting will decide what tasks in progress need their priority changed. Tasks will be assigned a deadline, and the team might need to change their behavior accordingly.

Service Delivery Review

Are we serving our clients well? Service delivery reviews will look at the system from the beneficiaries' point of view.

Department and team efficiency will be wasted if a client is not satisfied. This review will explore customer satisfaction in all aspects of the process, how well the team's resources are utilized, efficiency, communication, and delivery. The main goal is improving customer satisfaction by building trust with transparency.

Look at the last batch of work that was delivered to the client. Were they satisfied with what was delivered, how quickly it was delivered, and how it was delivered? Were they satisfied with the use of resources that you had available? If things went wrong, were they happy with how you handled the problem?

Risk Review

This conversation could happen at all levels within the organization. It should happen at every level. It is needed to assess how likely it is you might fail to deliver, either to end users or downstream components.

Finding risks ahead of time and taking the steps to remove those risks will improve the system's predictability. This will, in turn, increase profitability and trust.

The basic level of risk review is examining past failures like rework, blocked tasks, and missed SLAs. It is also done by identifying the causes and finding ways to stop these from happening in the future. Comprehensive planning will include speculating about future risks by having them based on input and experience.

Strategy Review

This examines market changes and looks at whether your current goals are serving needs and being optimized.

Are you really efficient? Is it running like a fine-tuned, well-oiled, streamlined machine? Are you doing the right things? Has anything changed due to market decisions? This meeting should review your company's strategy and make sure you are delivering the value that will serve as your goal.

Compare recent delivery times with market trends. Did you deliver efficiently enough to adapt? If there are problems between your ability to make changes and the pace of the market, then you might need to change markets or find new ways to optimize your process. Company executives are the best to answer these questions. They have all the input from customer service, sales, and marketing. This meeting could result in new guidelines on how to evaluate products that are aligned with the market's expectations.

Time-based

These cadences need to occur every day, week, quarterly, or annually. This is good for situations where there will be value by having frequent updates or those important non-urgent things that may not happen any other way.

Event-driven

It isn't written anywhere that these have to happen at normal intervals. It makes sense to link some of them to events. Risk reviews should be done monthly. They might be triggered by bad failures. Service delivery reviews should only be done twice a year if everything is going well. One might be triggered by failing to meet SLAs in a crucial area. Replenishment meetings might be held each week or sooner if there aren't a certain number of items in the input queue.

Doing things well and finding ways to be better are fundamental to any work. You have probably already set aside some meetings that may serve all these purposes. The value of these cadences is finding out if you are getting everything done and evaluating if you have any gaps.

Analytics and Metrics

A Kanban system will give an organization several simple, yet powerful metrics that are directly connected to benefits for the business. When it comes to Kanban, metrics focus on looking on "time to market" or "time to value," and using these things to see continuous improvement.

CFD – Cumulative Flow Diagram

This is a simple metric that will give a lot of information about the team and system capability at a glance.

This is a time-based plot of your cards as they move through your board. CFD will start to plot the amount of cards that are located in every stage of your value stream. These CFDs are normally plotted every day, but for boards that move faster, they can be plotted every hour.

The different colors on the board indicate the different workflow stages. The band height at different areas indicates how many cards were in that stage at that particular point.

The top band is normally your backlog where your work starts out, and the bottom is typically the completed work. With an actual physical board, you could have a tray or envelope that you place the completed cards. For a virtual board, they are placed into an archived status.

As a whole, the CFD lets you know the number of cards that have been moved in and out of every stage per time unit and the number of cards that traversed the board. The CFD slop also lets you know how your system's throughput is. The greater the slope, the better the throughput, which means the amount of cards that were delivered per time unit.

A CFD is a great information source on how your team is performing and will provide you with information about lead time, WIP, and bottlenecks.

CFD gives you the most comprehensive picture of your system's delivery ability. Since the majority of teams work with lots of different items and have different experiences and skill sets in its people, the CFD provides a composite picture of what a certain team can do, and then you can use that info to predict what can be delivered.

Cycle Time Control

Every single process will vary. If you write your signature five times, they may look similar, but not two of them will be exactly the same. There will be an inherent variation, but it will vary between predictable limits. While you are writing you name, if somebody bumps you, you will end up with an unusual variation because of a special cause.

There isn't any common cause variation. Take a Tennis player for example. If she has great control, most of the serves will be where she wants them. There is going to be a slight variation, but not much. If she doesn't have any control, the serves will go all over the place, making more variation. With Kanban, there aren't any special causes such as wind, or change of ball. There are common cause variations. This will end up causing a loss in service and easy points for opponent, and could end up costing her the game, which is expensive. Likewise, with the majority of processes, reducing common cause variations will save you money.

Control charts will help you to see the variation. Control charts will provide you with:

- o Performance data plotted over time.
- o Lower and upper statistical control limits that show you the acceptable boundaries of variations. You will normally see these drawn at a distance of three sigma from the mean.
- o A center-line, which is usually the average of all the data plotted and is also called the mean.

Since data is typically distributed, the process is in control when 99.7% of the data is within the plus or minus 3-sigma limit. Whenever you get data points that fall outside of this limit, the analysis needs to be performed to figure out and get rid of the data because of special causes. Then, through further process improvements, you can also reduce common cause variation. This will lead to substantial benefits, especially when it comes to the system's or team's predictability and how it can make reliable commitments about the delivery of service.

Cycle or Lead Time Distribution

When you look at the lead time distribution chart, it provides you with how often cards are completed at different values of cycle or lead time.

Average Cycle Time Chart

This chart will provide you with exactly what the name implies, the average time of a cycle trend over a certain period. While having averages isn't the best way to come up with predictions about certain items or sets, it will serve to provide you with helpful insights of the trend over a certain time period.

When you look at one of these charts, you will easily be able to see whether the cycle time is going up, bad, or going down, good. When you use a combination of the three cycle time charts, you will be able to quickly catch these types of trends and make the adjustments that you need to, so that cycle time doesn't increase.

Cycle times of your cards are the total amount of time that the card will spend on the board, which is also the total work time and wait time.

Flow Efficiency Chart

This chart will highlight the critical impact of your system's wait stages. The majority of people won't realize that all of the value streams will have a number of wait stages. This could be handoffs between the different stages or the wait that is created by external resource needs.

Wait stages affect flow efficiency and cycle time. The bigger your wait times are, the lower your flow efficiency is going to be. Some of the best work teams that use a Kanban system will see a flow efficiency of 25 to 40 percent. This statistic means that around 60 to 85 percent of the time work is waiting for somebody to pull it, or for some form of input.

This measurement can be easily enabled in a Kanban system, and it gives you a lot of insight into your efficiency. It will help you to figure out how it can be improved.

Blocker Analysis Chart

When you use tools like WIP Limits, as well as visual cues like WIP Limit violations and Blockers, your system will highlight various impediments in the flow of your system. A blocker chart will help you to highlight a few of the root causes of the reason why cards are getting blocked, and you will be able to deal with these root causes.

The longer you cards stay blocked, the longer you cycle time will end up being and lower your efficiency. The analysis will help the team to figure out how to reduce blocking and better the flow and cycle time.

Throughput Chart

Throughput tells you how many cards are delivered during each time unit. This is a great chart to help you to understand the team's capabilities and make the best commitments to the customer about the amount of work that the team can provide in a certain amount of time.

Predictive Analytics

Overall, through using a Kanban system, you can easily and quickly come up with a graph of your team's performance data so that you can communicate clearly with your customers and the stakeholders that your system is demonstrating capabilities, and how you predict the future of delivery to look. You will also have an associated level of confidence and probability.

You can use an electronic Kanban tool like SwiftKanban to automate the collection of data and generate metrics. These types of advanced Kanban tools will provide you with predictive analytics capabilities using things like a Monte Carlo simulation to help further empower your team to make better decisions based upon the analysis of have you have previously performed.

WIP Limits

One property of Kanban, which is work-in-progress, is limited. A way to limit WIP is to match your team's capacity for development. You would normally set the WIP limit for each column or workflow stage. It is acceptable to set limits for each person or team. Setting a limit for any column doesn't mean you can't add another task in that particular column. Instead, it just means that when one limit is reached, the entire team needs to take responsibility and understand why this happened. They need to realize that they can improve and keep it from occurring again in the future.

WIP limits are important because they help improve throughput. They also reduce all the work that gets "nearly done." They force the person or team to stay focused on smaller tasks. Looking at WIP limits from a fundamental perspective encourages a "done" culture. WIP limits assure that bottlenecks and blockers are easier to see. Teams can work together around issues to understand them so they can resolve the problem that is causing the bottleneck. When the blocks are removed, work will start to flow once more. These benefits will bring value to the customers. Setting WIP limits is a great tool in development.

When you are in the development stage, it is easy to think about jumping from one task to another. When you are working on two problems at the same time, you have to switch between the two or transfer work to another teammate. Jumping from one issue to another is not free. It lessens focus and takes a lot of time. It is always better to work through one problem instead of starting and then not being able to complete a new task. WIP limits discourage people from getting in the way of their own flow.

WIP limits will show areas of overload or constant idleness. They will show the team their inefficiencies throughout the whole process instead of one area they work in.

When you set WIP limits, you need to ask two crucial questions:

1. How many people are on your team?
2. How many items can they work on at one time?

There are no secret formulas set for establishing WIP limits. It is normal that limits might be wrong, to begin with. You should never expect the limit to stay where you put it. They will need to be adjusted from time to time. You shouldn't stress over setting the initial limits.

Setting WIP limits will help your team focus on quality, completion, and making the right decisions. It also allows them to enable a pull model, get feedback to limit waste because of incorrect assumptions and rework, measure the number of tasks that could be done at one time, get a flow of work that will be delivered on time, avoid distraction by switching tasks and reduces multitasking.

Limiting WIP won't solve every problem your team might face. Not limiting WIP guarantees that you will fall victim to wasting time. If you don't have WIP limits, you will see that process improvements will be a lot slower. Teams that have used this from the start have seen growth and have delivered great results.

You can customize your Kanban board template by using Kanban Tool. To set up your WIP limits, go to "Setting," and then click "Board editor." Next, click the pencil icon in order to edit your WIP limit. Now all you have to do is fill in the "Task count limit."

Kanban Tool is an enterprising software that will allow real-time collaboration and allows you to boost your team's productivity.

Helpful Tips

Bottleneck

Has your team ever finished a project on time without paying any overtime or having any delays?

Bottlenecks are the main reason projects are delayed. Budgets are gone over because of the cost of delays, and the entire process has been turned into something unpredictable.

You don't have to fight the symptoms. All you need to do is an analysis and set up some prevention measures in order to save the process.

Use Kanban to help you analyze and identify process bottlenecks and figure out a flow that is predictable, and you will be in complete control.

The easiest way to define a bottleneck is, it's a stage of work that has more requests than what is possible to process at maximum capacity. This will create an interruption in the workflow and causes delays throughout the entire process.

Even if the work stage can operate at maximum capacity, there is no way to process all the work fast enough to get them to the next stage without creating any delays.

The bottleneck could be a certain department, person, computer, or the entire process. Normal bottlenecks are quality review and software testing.

The bad news is, most bottlenecks are only realized after a block in the workflow has been created.

There are effective but simple tools within Kanban that will help you spot a bottleneck and stop work congestion.

If you notice that your process often operates in bursts and has a tendency to be unpredictable instead of flowing smoothly, you will find a bottleneck somewhere within the system.

The main issue is finding it and figuring out a good countermeasure. There are several analysis tools within Kaban to help you find a bottleneck.

There are three easy steps to find a bottleneck:

The first one is to visualize. Keep track of work by using task cards on a board. This will show when work begins to pile up. This is the good indicator of a problem, which is usually a bottleneck.

The second one is to map out activities and queues. If you can separate activities and queues onto a Kanban board, you will be able to see how much time work has been waiting in queue before it moves into an activity. If this particular queue continues to grow faster than the work moves, you have a bottleneck.

The third way is to measure the cycle time within each stage. Measuring the cycle time of each stage will allow you to create a cycle time diagram. Just by looking at the diagram, it will show you where the cards are spending the majority of their time. Also, if these stages are in queue, you might have found your bottleneck.

What should you do in order to deal with bottlenecks? You should be able to resolve any bottleneck by putting more people or resources on a particular process or stage. This might mean hiring more quality assurance testers in order to get a better production flow.

What should you do if the bottleneck needs a scarce resource or an expert that is hard to come by? In many cases, these costs are just too high. But you should never leave a bottleneck untreated. This can cost you more money than fixing it.

There are ways you can contain the bottleneck:

You can't ever leave it alone. This will create a ripple effect that will disrupt the entire flow of the process. The bottleneck needs to be loaded at full capacity.

Try to alleviate the strain the bottleneck is causing. Work needs to arrive at the bottleneck in the best form possible. If the review itself is a bottleneck, make sure that quality control is done from the very beginning. The reviewed work needs to be flawless. Every error a reviewer finds will cost more money and time.

Manage limits within WIP. If there are liberal limits in the progress of the bottleneck and there is switching of context, you need to think about lowering the WIP limit. If the progress doesn't have a WIP limit, you might want to think about setting one.

Make batches of process work. The operation might take less time if you were to take time to organize similar work into batches. Be careful, because the bigger the batch, the larger the risk. The main rule is, smaller batches will always work better, but sometimes you must make compromises.

You might have to use more resources and people. If it is possible, you might think about increasing the bottleneck to help speed up the entire process. Just watch out. When resources within the system are distributed elsewhere, a different bottleneck might pop up somewhere else.

Seven Wastes of Lean

Getting rid of useless activities is extremely important for a successful company. This is a main component of Lean thinking, and it will help you increase your profits.

This idea originated from Taiichi Ohno. He ran the Toyota Production System and is thought of as the founding father of Lean manufacturing. His entire career was based on establishing an efficient and solid work process.

He found three roadblocks that can negatively influence work processes. These are Mura, or unevenness, Muri, or overburden, and Muda, or wasteful activities.

He figured out seven types of waste by using deep analysis. He called these the seven Mudas. They became a practice to help optimize resources and reduce costs.

What exactly is waste or Muda in Lean? Waste is an activity that uses resources but doesn't bring any value to the customer.

Activities that create values for customers are just a little portion of the entire process. This is the main reason businesses need to focus on getting rid of activities that are wasteful. By doing this, companies will be able to see ways to improve their complete performance.

An important note here: You can't get rid of every wasteful activity. Some are actually needed.

Software testing is not something that customers want to pay for. You might end up with a poor-quality product if you don't incorporate it. This will then have a bad impact on your performance financially. This creates two main types of waste:

Needed waste: This type of waste doesn't add value but is needed to do things in a timely manner. These activities could be reporting, planning, or testing.

Pure waste: This type of waste is not needed and doesn't add value. If something doesn't bring you value, it should be removed immediately. Any length of wait could be figured in as pure waste.

Getting rid of activities that are wasteful is critical if you want your company to have success. Waste can decrease how satisfied your employees are, decrease the quality of products, increase costs for customers, and lower your profits. You have to find the activities that don't add any value and fix the process where they are or get rid of them totally.

There are seven main areas in the Lean theory where you can find Muda activities, also known as the seven wastes of Lean.

Transportation waste is when you move materials or resources around, and it still doesn't add any value to your product. Moving materials excessively could cost your business a lot of money and damage the quality of your product. Sometimes, transportation might cause you to pay more for machinery, space, and time.

Too much inventory is usually the result of a business holding on to inventory "just in case" they might need it. Companies will sometimes have too much stock to try and meet the demand that they aren't expecting. They try to protect themselves from delays with production or possible low-quality production. These inventories usually won't meet the needs of customers and don't add any value to the company. They just depreciate costs and increase storage.

Motion waste is any type of moving of machinery or employees. These are both unnecessary and complicated. They might extend production time, and possibly cause injuries. The main goal is to do what you need to in order to create a process where workers don't have a complicated process to do their jobs.

Waiting is the easiest to recognize. Anytime tasks or goods aren't moving, waiting waste happens. You can identify it easily since time being lost is very easy to detect. Examples of waiting waste include: forms or documents waiting to be approved by supervisors, equipment needing to be fixed but sitting in the mechanic's shop, or goods needing to be delivered.

Overproduction turns to Muda when you have more merchandise than the customer is willing to buy. Producing more than the customer demands will lead to more cost. Overproduction will trigger the other wastes to happen. This is the main reason tasks or products are in need of more transportation, more motion, and longer wait times. If a defect happens during overproduction, this means your team has to work more units.

Overprocessing is a waste that reflects work which didn't bring more value or brought more value than was needed. These things could be adding more features to a product that no one will use. They just increase the cost for your business. If a computer software company creates apps or games that nobody knows how to play or wants to play, there is no value to that. They are just using resources and increasing the price of the computer. These are things consumers don't want to pay for.

Defects could cause employees to work more, or lead to scrap. Normally, defective work needs to go back through production, and this costs more time. In most cases, reworking of an area is needed and comes with the cost of tools and labor.

These seven types of waste can be very toxic to businesses. You can look at them as a way to improve processes and optimize resources. In every business, these forms of waste will have many different aspects.

Variability

A simple definition of variability is the lack of fixed pattern or consistency. It can be a liability to change or vary. Variability can cause more work and longer lead times. It can create a larger need for slack in resources that are not bottlenecked to help cope with the flow of work throughout the entire process. Variability within the size of the requirement and in how much effort is needed on delivery, integration, testing, coding, design, and analysis can affect the process and costs of running software development.

There are two types of variability: external and internal.

Internal sources are controlled by the operating system. These can also be called chance cause variations. Here, chance implies that the variation is random and the direct consequence of the process design. It doesn't say the randomness is distributed evenly. Changing the process design can affect the variations' shape, spread, and means of distribution. When we look at the name "chance cause", we can tell that while one certain cause might not be clear, a set of opportunities and causes to fix them already exist. An example of a chance cause variation could be the amount of bugs that get created on each line of code as required by each task or amount of time. The number, spread, and how the bug is distributed is affected by changing the process and tools, like doing unit tests, constant integration, and doing peer code reviews.

External sources are things that occur which the workers or supervisors can't control. These are also called assignable causes. External sources need different approaches in order to manage them. They aren't affected by policies, but you can put in place a process to handle them. This is usually handled by risk management. The word "assignable" means that a person or group of people should be able to find the problem and be able to describe it. These variations can't be controlled by a team but can be predicted. Plans can be made and processed, created to deal with them easily.

The main thing to remember is that the problem is easy to see, and action is taken to properly define the source.

Here are some internal sources of variability:

Since work items use stories or cases by decomposing the requirements, it creates the chance cause variation. Instead of using index cards to show requirements and increase the variation, changing the policy to follow a story structure can decrease time from five weeks to just one-and-a-half days.

It takes different amounts of time to complete different types of work. Measuring and managing completion of different-sized items can increase variability and reduces predictability. When you use techniques to find the work item types, you can change the spread and mean of variability and help the predictability for all types of work.

Class of service mix will manage service classes the same way work items do. You might incorporate a policy where these limits have to be strictly enforced, or choose to loosen up and allow an item to fill a slot for a certain date or time when there isn't enough demand for these items. You can switch the policies around during different times to help with the total economic outcome and make sure the system stays predictable.

Rework from either bugs being dealt with before its release or defects in production which displaces customer work will affect variability. If they happen during a predictable rate and are sized right, then the system can handle them. This is usually not the case. Rework that happens because of bugs increases the lead times, will increase the variation spread and reduces throughput. The best way to reduce variability because of defects is to pursue the highest quality with extremely low defects.

Irregular flow can be avoided by allowing time to complete most work. Irregular flow can be created by both external and internal sources. Predictability will breed trust.

When you can rigorously follow the different works in process, it will limit the randomness and classes of items of the different sizes and risk profiles. The larger the variability, the more you need to buffer. More buffering creates more work in process. The more work in process means it takes longer for work to flow through the system. This is the desired outcome since customers, managers, and owners value predictability more over chance.

Here are some external sources of variability:

These sources of variability are found in places that aren't controlled by software development or project management. These might happen due to server failures, power outages, other team members, or environmental outages.

Badly written requirements, vision, no strategic planning, badly defined business plans, or other information might cause a worker to be unable to make decisions so they can't complete their work. This item will become blocked because it is unable to make a decision. Now, new information is needed to fix the situation so the worker can make good decisions that will allow the work to flow to completion. Requirements ambiguity, just like other sources, can be influenced but never controlled.

Expedite requests are created due to external events like a customer order or because there was a breakdown in the company's internal process. Expediting in engineering is bad. It harms the predictability of requests. It can increase lead time and spreads the variability and reduces the throughput. Expediting is not desirable even when trying to generate value. Normally, within the Kanban system, expediting requests makes the delivery clear and will motivate the need to set strict limits. They need to be eliminated over time.

Environment availability is an assignable cause variation.

Some teams will see external sources as blockers. Relying on the environment and specialists like DBAs, deployment and system engineers are all blockers. Most organizations don't have any risk management capabilities.

There are two approaches to help reduce the irregularity that blocked items create:

1. Define higher limits and accept longer lead times without predictability.
2. Keep tight limits on work in process. Keep sizes low and resist longer lead times with lower predictability.

Doing and Done

An easy and simple improvement that you can make to your Kanban system is by separating states into "doing" and "done." This will give you a more accurate visualization of the actual state of a certain task. It adds a lot to the granularity of the metrics and is important to enable the move from a push to a pull mindset.

Let's say that a team has two columns: development and test. When a developer finishes the first story, they will push it into the test column. But the system is actually lying. Just because the developer has placed it into test, doesn't mean that the testing has started.

Now, consider that the development and test columns were both broken down into doing and done. Once the developer has finished the first story, they placed it into the done section of development. This will signal the testers that they can now pull the first story into the doing column of test. If large lists of tasks start to build up in the development, done column, then we can easily spot a bottleneck emerging in the before test. If, after some time, we notice that stories spend too much time in this column, it will trigger us to take a look into the root cause of this.

You could also choose to assign these names to the columns:
- Development
- Ready for Test
- Test
- Ready for Acceptance

The truth is that the difference is only intellectual. Aesthetically, doing and done is preferred, mainly because it provides less apparent states, and you can assign WIP limits in the doing and done column.

Conclusion

Thanks for making it through to the end of *Kanban*. I hope it was informative and able to provide you with all of the tools you need to achieve your goals, whatever they may be.

The next step is to start using the information you have learned. Kanban is a very helpful tool for everybody. It increases the efficiency of just about any task, so try it out to see if it works for your team. Whether you're a software developer or a project manager, Kanban can help.

Finally, if you found this book useful in any way, a review on Amazon is always appreciated!

Check out more books by James Edge

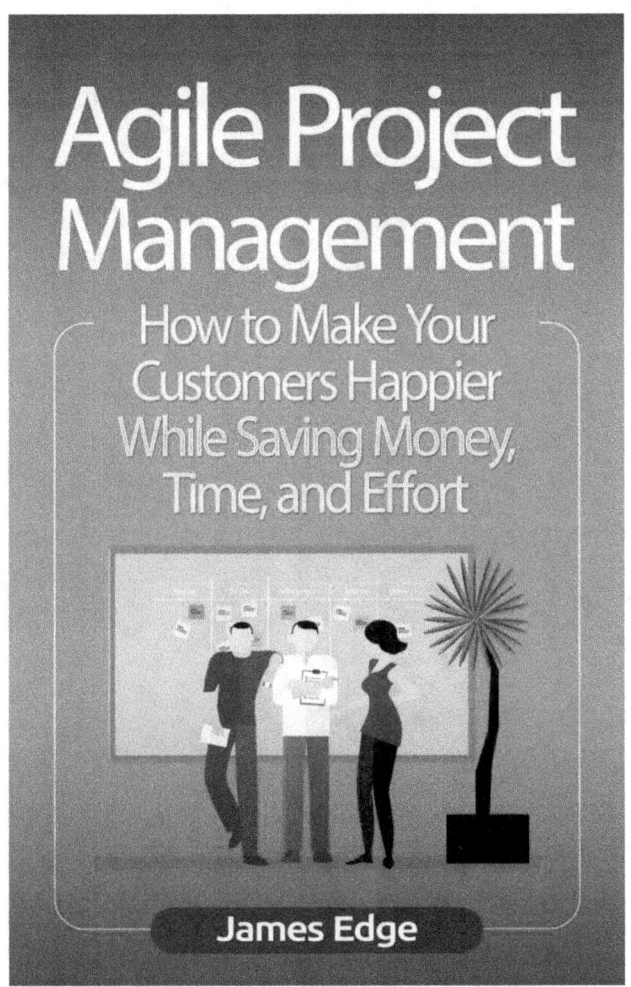

www.ingramcontent.com/pod-product-compliance
Lightning Source LLC
Chambersburg PA
CBHW071420220526
45469CB00004B/1359